Fiddle Time Duets

30 progressive duets for violin

Kathy and David Blackwell

Welcome to **Fiddle Time Duets**. You'll find:

- duets using easy 1st position finger patterns to pieces that use 3rd position
- some duets with parts of equal difficulty and some with a harder part suitable for a teacher or more advanced student
- an additional six mini duet warm-ups exploring different techniques and skills
- a variety of musical styles, from classical and folk repertoire to original compositions
- material suitable for both sight-reading and concert performance
- an ideal resource to help develop ensemble skills
- the perfect companion to the books in the *Fiddle Time* series.

OXFORD
UNIVERSITY PRESS

Great Clarendon Street, Oxford OX2 6DP, England.
This collection and each individual work within it © Oxford University Press 2023.
Unauthorized arrangement or photocopying of this copyright material is ILLEGAL.

Kathy and David Blackwell have asserted their right under the Copyright, Designs and Patents Act, 1988, to be identified as the Composers of this Work.

Impression: 1

ISBN 978-0-19-356519-7

Music and text origination by Julia Bovee
Printed in Great Britain

Welcome to **Fiddle Time Duets**.

Here you'll find 30 attractive and progressive violin duets to enjoy, from arrangements of classical and folk music to imaginative original compositions. There are also six mini duet warm-ups that explore different techniques and skills.

The duets in each section correspond approximately to the technical levels of the books in the *Fiddle Time* series: *Starters, Joggers, Runners, Sprinters,* and *Solo Time for Violin Book 1*. **Fiddle Time Duets** is thus an invaluable resource for students at various stages of learning, from an established beginner (approx. Initial/Grade 1) to Grade 3–4 level. Some duets have parts of equal difficulty, while some have a harder part (usually the lower) suitable for a teacher or more advanced student, making it a useful resource for students at different stages of learning to play together.

The book also provides ideal sight-reading material and great repertoire for concert performance. You'll find a range of keys, styles, techniques, and much opportunity to develop ensemble skills in this attractive collection. A range of free resources, including some additional duet material, is free to download at www.kathyanddavidblackwell.co.uk.

So find a duet partner and enjoy exploring the diverse range of music in **Fiddle Time Duets!**

This book is dedicated to Clare, Iain, and Angus, with love.

Kathy and David Blackwell

Contents

Mini Duet Warm-ups

These six short duets explore different violin techniques and skills. Each has an easier part (top), and a harder part (lower). Choose a part to suit and enjoy some fun warm-ups.

Jazzy jogging rhythm
top: short bow strokes, middle of the bow; *lower*: high and low 3rd finger

Raindrops
top: LH pizz. in middle position, or RH pizz.; *lower*: *détaché* bowing, low 2nd finger

Scale the heights
top: descending D major scale; *lower*: 3rd position

stay in 3rd position

On the move

top: LH pizz., pluck Es in first position and Gs in middle position; *lower*: low 2nd finger, staccato bowing

Smooth talking

both parts: legato playing, two-note slurs, high and low 2nd fingers

Pizza toppings

top: holding fingers down in G major chord pattern; *lower*: crossing over 2, 3, and 4 strings

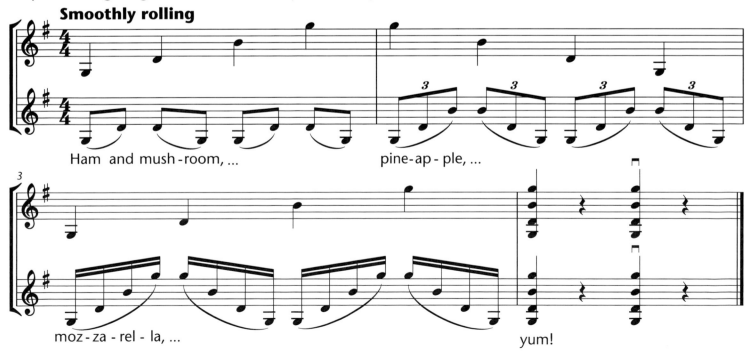

Ham and mush-room, ...   pine-ap-ple, ...

moz-za-rel-la, ...   yum!

1. Let's Celebrate!

KB & DB

f
(*2nd time faster!*)

f

(*tremolo*)

(*tremolo*)

2. Bird Song

KB & DB

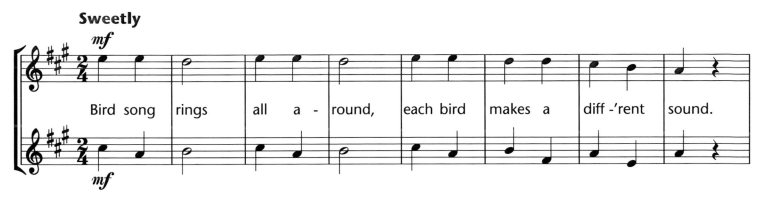

Bird song rings all a - round, each bird makes a diff -'rent sound.

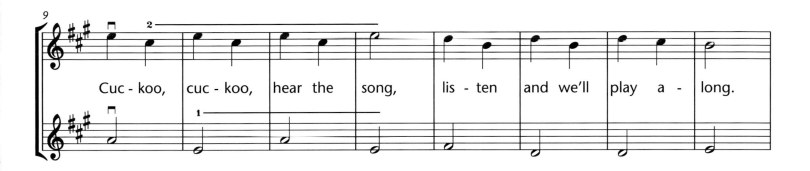

Cuc - koo, cuc - koo, hear the song, lis - ten and we'll play a - long.

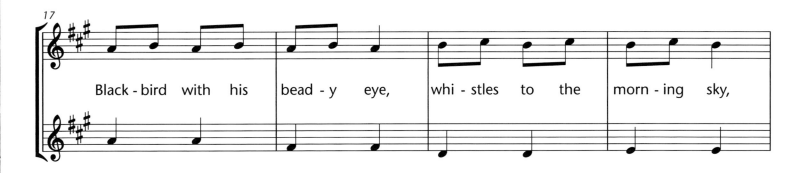

Black - bird with his bead - y eye, whi - stles to the morn - ing sky,

barn owl in the mid - night blue, gent - ly coos 'Tu - whit, tu - whoo'!

3. Run for your life!

KB & DB

With excitement

accel.

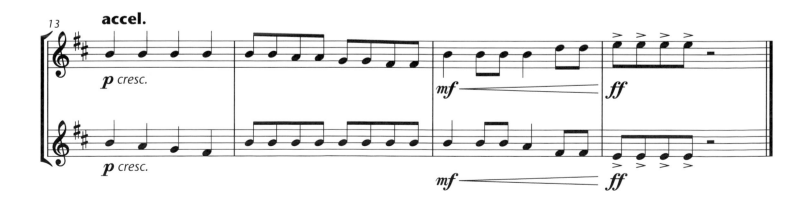

4. Donkeys love carrots

Les ânes aiment les carottes

Belgian folk tune
arr. KB & DB

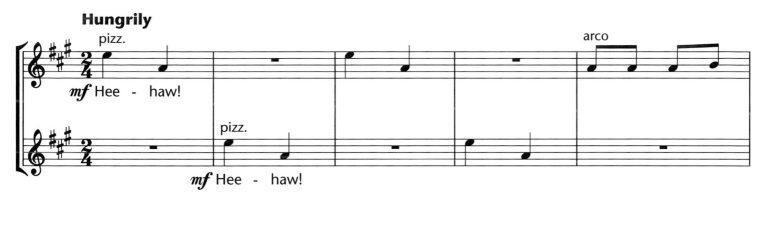

You can also try playing the pizzicato notes with left-hand 4th finger. The words of this folk tune (top part bar 5, lower part bar 7) are: 'Donkeys like to munch on carrots. Carrots don't like that at all. Hee-haw, hee-haw, listen to the donkeys' call!'

5. Lani sem kupil

Last year I bought

Slovenian folk tune
arr. KB & DB

This song is about greedy people who always want more, no matter how many presents they're given.

6. Silver Moon Boat

Xiao Yin Chuan

Chinese folk tune
arr. KB & DB

Gently rocking

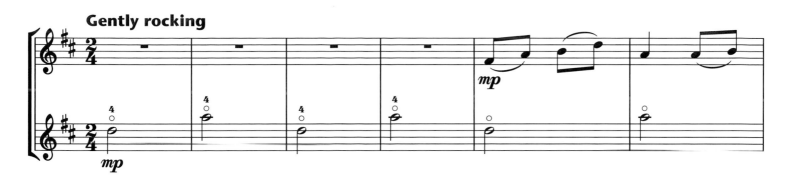

slower

7. Buttered Peas

Pwt ar y Bys

Welsh folk tune
arr. KB & DB

Swap parts on the repeats.

8. Sharing a Surprise!

from Symphony No. 94 (*The Surprise*)

Joseph Haydn (1732–1809)
arr. KB & DB

9. Lullaby for Angus

KB & DB

10. Niño Manuelito

Peruvian folk tune
arr. KB & DB

In this duet players take turns—the tune and accompaniment pass between the two players. The title means 'Child Emmanuel', a name for Jesus.

11. Sort of Rocky

KB & DB

Confidently

12. Eh soom boo kawaya

Nigerian folk tune
arr. KB & DB

This folk song, traditional to the Ibibio people of Nigeria, loosely translates as: fishermen are out fishing and when it starts to rain they have to paddle faster!

13. Simple Gifts

Joseph Brackett (1797–1882)
arr. KB & DB

14. Melody

from String Quartet No. 13, Op. 130, 4th movement

Ludwig van Beethoven (1770–1827)
arr. KB & DB

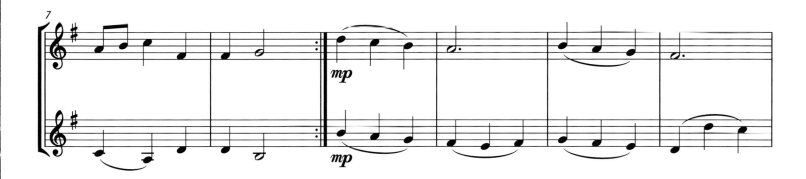

15. One, two, three, four, paper hat

Een, twee, drie, vier, hoedje van papier

Dutch folk tune
arr. KB & DB

16. Minuet

No. 1 from *Six Minuets*, K105

W. A. Mozart (1756–91)
arr. KB & DB

Swap parts on the repeats.

17. Prleška

Slovenian folk tune
arr. KB & DB

This humorous song from Prlekija, eastern Slovenia, is about a boy who does not want to go to school and instead wants to be a farmer.

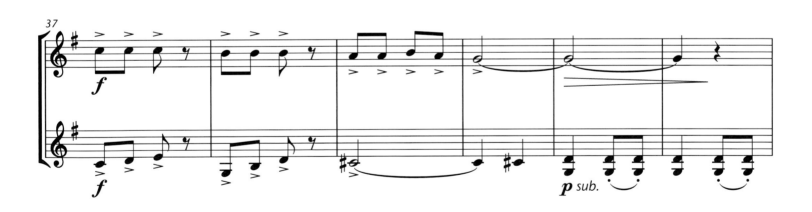

18. Rondeau

from String Quartet, Op. 1 No. 6

Joseph Bologne, Chevalier de Saint-Georges (1745–99)
arr. KB & DB

19. Air

Henry Purcell (1659–95)
arr. KB & DB

20. Prince of Denmark's March

Jeremiah Clarke (1674–1707)
arr. KB & DB

The trills are optional.

21. Dance

adapted from 12 German Dances, WoO 13 No. 9

Ludwig van Beethoven (1770–1827)
arr. KB & DB

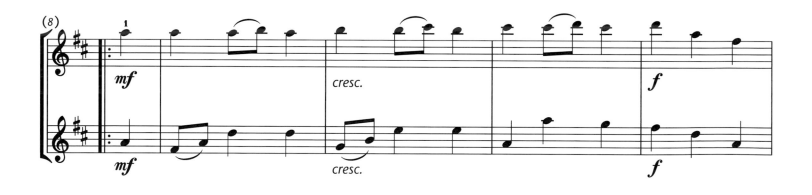

Swap parts on the repeats.

22. Allegretto

from Sonata for Violin and Keyboard, Op. 1 No. 3

Francesca Lebrun (1756–91)
arr. KB & DB

for Angus

23. Arpeggio Games

KB & DB

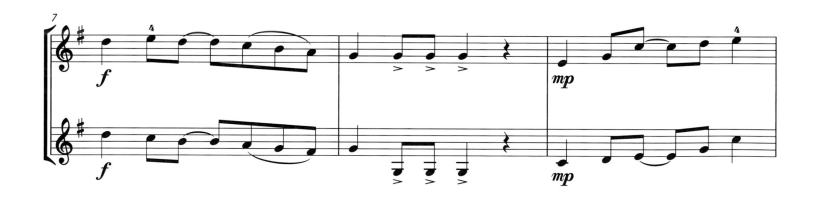

24. Hornpipe

from *Minuets etc. for the Violin and Harpsichord*, Book 2

Ignatius Sancho (1729–80)
arr. KB & DB

Allegro

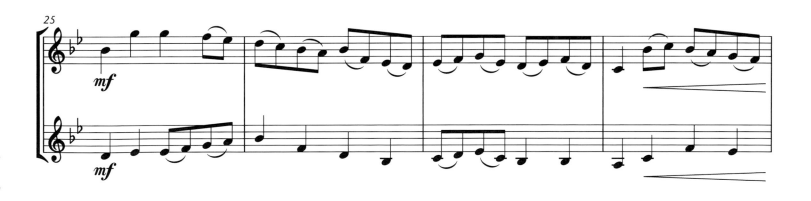

25. Early one morning

English folk tune
arr. KB & DB

26. Ma Yofus

How Beautiful (also known as *Tanz, Tanz Yidelekh*)

Klezmer folk tune
arr. KB & DB

27. Latin nights

Tango

KB & DB

28. Gavotta

from Violin Sonata, Op. 2 No. 9, RV 16

Antonio Vivaldi (1678–1741)
arr. KB & DB

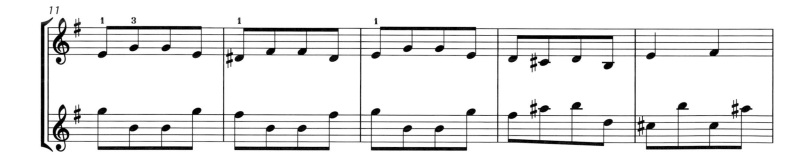

29. Celebration Canon

KB & DB

30. Reflections

Mirror duet

KB & DB

Player 1

To play *Reflections*, place the music on a table or flat surface. Player 1 plays from the beginning to the end, while Player 2 looks at the music upside down and plays from the end back to the beginning. Follow the dynamics placed below the stave. The music acts as a mirror in that the notes of Player 1 are played upside down and in reverse order by Player 2.